The 4 Things You Must Know

to Make Money While You Sleep

Book 1 in the Internet Marketing FAST Series

Copyright and Enquiries

Comments or enquiries may be left in the *Contact Me* page at

https://superaffiliatechallenge.com/contact-me

Contents

Table of Figures

The 4 Things You Must Know

to Make Money While You Sleep

Internet Marketing

There is no better model for making money while you sleep than internet marketing. This is because

- Your website is available to make automatic sales 24 hours a day, 7 days a week, 52 weeks (and one day) a year
- Your customers can live anywhere in the world, including countries that are awake while you are asleep.

The 4 Things

The four things you must know to get started in internet marketing are how to:

1. Select a Niche
2. Register a Domain Name
3. Open a Web Host Account
4. Build a Website.

These won't create a profitable internet business for you by themselves but they are the foundation that you will need first.

In the bricks and mortar world, these are equivalent to:

1. Deciding what business you want to be in, such as opening a restaurant
2. Getting and registering a name for your restaurant
3. Leasing premises
4. Building, equipping and decorating the restaurant.

At this stage, no one knows about your new business and you don't have any customers or income.

The 4 Things You Must Know

The big difference is the cost.

For the bricks and mortar business, it's considerable.

For the internet marketing business, it's trivial.

The 4 Things You Must Know

to Make Money While You Sleep

First Thing: Select a Niche

Internet Marketing Starts with Selecting a Niche

Figure 1: Selecting a Niche: It Isn't That Hard

If you are starting any sort of business, whether it's bricks and mortar or an online business, the first question you have to ask yourself is "What is my business all about?"

In the online world, it's called choosing your niche and, although it's very important, bear in mind that it may be just the first of many online businesses that you are going to own.

The 4 Things You Must Know
to Make Money While You Sleep

Unlike the bricks and mortar world, it costs very little to start an online business so the chances are that you will eventually own several.

This of course has the advantage that each one only needs to earn a small amount for it to all add up to a decent income. And if just one of them takes off, you can do very well indeed.

But it also means don't hesitate too much.

Avoid "paralyses by analysis" and jump right in, even if it's just for the learning experience.

So How Do You Select a Niche?

There are two ways to select a niche for your online business:

1. Choose something that you are knowledgeable, even passionate about. In other words, a familiar subject.
2. Choose something that gets a lot of searches and has a large number of related products. In other words, a popular subject.

Familiar Subject as Internet Niche: Advantage

The advantage of a familiar subject is that you are going to be writing a lot of content around it and that will be easier if you are already knowledgeable and passionate about it.

The aim of your website is to provide useful and valuable information about your subject to your visitors so that you become an authority in your niche. You can do this by writing articles that address different aspects of your subject (and which also target keywords aimed at getting you ranked in the search engines; don't worry, I cover Search Engine Optimization (SEO) and Free and Paid Traffic in my *Affiliate Marketing FAST* training

The 4 Things You Must Know

to Make Money While You Sleep

course. You can register your no-obligation interest in the course and qualify for some free gifts at:

https://imfasttraining.com/expression-of-interest/

You might also write an e-book on your niche that you give away on your website in exchange for your visitor's name and email address so that you can subsequently send offers to them. This is called a lead magnet.

You don't even have to write the book yourself. For a very low price, you can buy PLR (Private Label Rights) to a book that has already been written for your niche. PLR means you can do anything you want with it, including making changes to the content, creating a new cover image and claiming authorship.

Alternatively, you can use an AI facility such as ChatGPT to write your e-book for you. There's a right and wrong way to go about this and I cover how to do it properly in the training course Affiliate Marketing FAST.

For extra income, you can publish your book on Amazon both as an e-book and a paperback. It's free to do so and can create an extra income stream. I'll explain how to do this in my *Creating and Publishing Your First Book on Amazon* training course. You can register your no-obligation interest in the course and qualify for some free gifts at:

https://thebookinside.com/register-your-interest/

Familiar Subject as Internet Niche: Disadvantage

The disadvantage of this approach is that while you may be passionate about a subject, if no one else is, then you won't get much in the way of visitors so all your good work in writing articles will be wasted.

The 4 Things You Must Know
to Make Money While You Sleep

Just because you're passionate about collecting old bottle caps or mapping the far side of the moon doesn't mean that visitors will flock to your specialized website or that you can make an income out of it.

Popular Subject as Internet Niche: Advantage

By choosing a niche that has a lot of searches and associated products, you increase the chances that, if your business is successful, you can make a lot of money from it.

For example, "weight loss" is one of the most searched for terms on the internet and has a ton of products associated with it, from diet books to treadmills.

So is it a good niche to be in?

For a startup business, probably not.

Popular Subject as Internet Niche: Disadvantage

The disadvantage of a popular subject is, well, its popularity. It means that the competition is intense.

A Google search for "weight loss" will bring up over 1 billion results!

And all of them will have been in business for much longer than you. Every keyword you can think of will already be the subject of other websites.

Your chances of making it to page 1 of Google, Bing or Yahoo through SEO are pretty much zero and if you're not on page 1, you might as well be invisible.

Yes, you can pay for ads, and I'll examine that option in detail further down the track, but for the uninitiated, it's a rapid way to spend money with no return.

The 4 Things You Must Know

to Make Money While You Sleep

What to Do?

Figure 2: Affiliate Marketing

Clearly, your best bet is to find something that you're knowledgeable about (or at least interested in) that will have a reasonable number of related searches but doesn't have an insane amount of competition and has associated products that you can sell.

What we are talking about here is selling products as an affiliate. That is, selling someone else's products that are related to your niche and you earn a commission. This is probably the best model for starting out with a money-making blog. Other models are advertising on your blog, drop-shipping products bought wholesale (e-commerce) and, of course, the ultimate of developing and selling your own products for 100% of the profit.

I will be covering all of these models as we proceed through this journey.

How to Select a (Profitable) Niche

We've covered the considerations involved in selecting a niche.

But you probably want to know exactly HOW to go about it.

Well, it's all about:

Keyword Research

There, you knew I'd get technical sooner or later, didn't you?

You see, the thing you want to do with your website is to rank highly in the search engines for particular keywords related to your niche.

Which means you need to find keywords (and note that while we call them "words" we actually mean phrases, so that, for example, "exercise routines for seniors" is a "keyword") that have a good number of searches but not so much competition.

But how do we find out?

Start with Your Niche Idea

Let's say you're a bike rider and like many bike riders, you spend a lot of money on your passion. This could include the actual bikes themselves, ancillary equipment such as group sets, lights and bike computers, along with specialized clothing. These could include knicks, jerseys, socks, cleated shoes and so on.

The 4 Things You Must Know
to Make Money While You Sleep

Or even if you're not a rider yourself, you've noticed others and have decided that something to do with bikes could be a good niche to be in.

Your first niche decision is:

Broad or Narrow?

You need to decide whether your niche should be broad or narrow.

There are a lot of firmly held opinions on this matter, so I'll try to cover the essentials that you need to consider.

The advantage of a broad niche is that it is less limiting. And you can divide it into sections that represent sub-niches or "topics". You can write a series of articles addressing just one topic at a time. These are called "topic clusters".

The advantage of a narrow niche is that you can devote all of your efforts to it and eventually be seen as the go-to specialist for that niche.

Sticking with bike riding, an example of a broad niche would be "cycling" or "bike riding" and examples of a narrow niche could be "road bikes" or (narrower still) "road bike clothing".

Refine It with Keyword Research

Keywords are simply terms that people are using to find products on the internet. Someone enters that term into a search engine (such as Google) and sees many pages of relevant results from different websites.

Your aim is for your site to be found on page 1 of the results pages so that people click on it and have the opportunity to buy the products you are promoting.

The 4 Things You Must Know
to Make Money While You Sleep

Your first job is to find keywords that people are searching for but without too much competition from other websites in the same market.

You will use a keyword research tool to do this.

Google "keyword research tool" to find out what is currently available. There are paid tools like Semrush and Moz but you might want to start out with something free.

Try Ryan Robinson's Free Keyword Research Tool at https://www.ryrob.com/keyword-tool/.

The 4 Things You Must Know
to Make Money While You Sleep

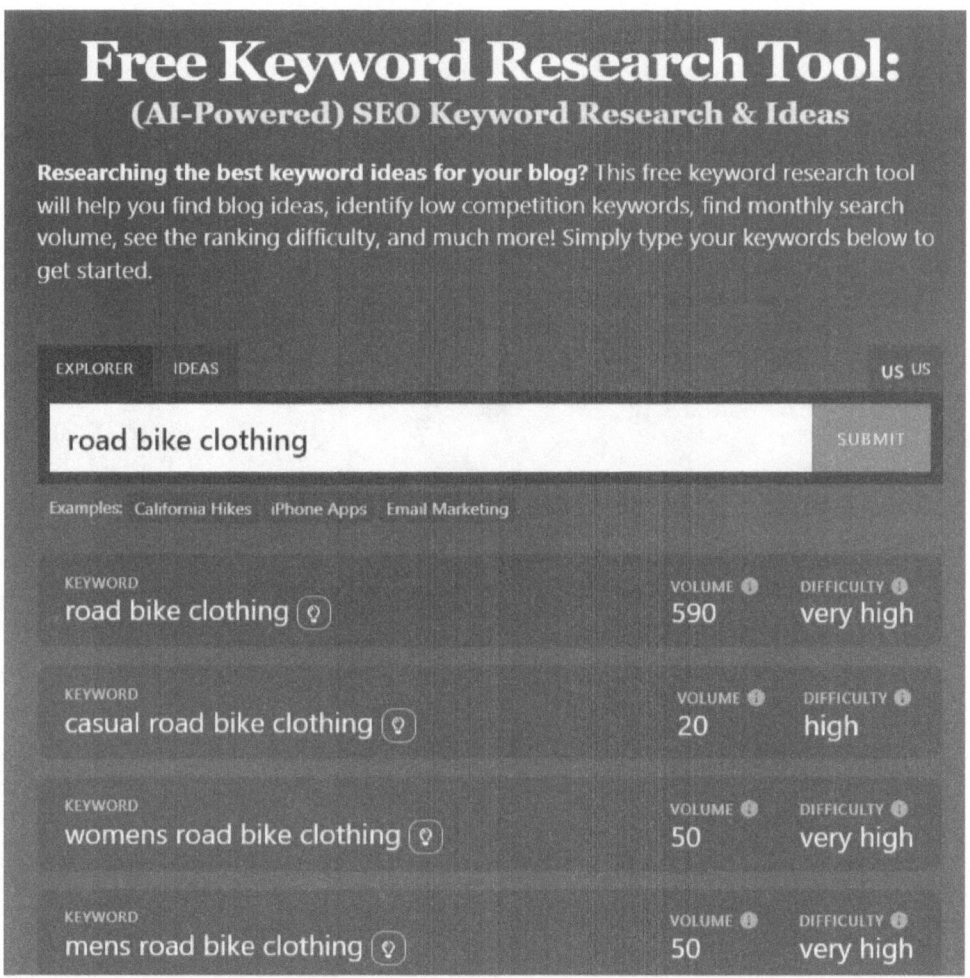

Figure 3: Keyword Research Road Bike Clothing

Have a look at road bike clothing above.

The keyword tool tells us that the monthly search volume is 590 (quite low) but that the difficulty is very high, meaning that there's a lot of competition. This is the opposite of what we want.

The 4 Things You Must Know
to Make Money While You Sleep

This doesn't mean that the niche is bad, just that keyword. Let's refine it a bit further.

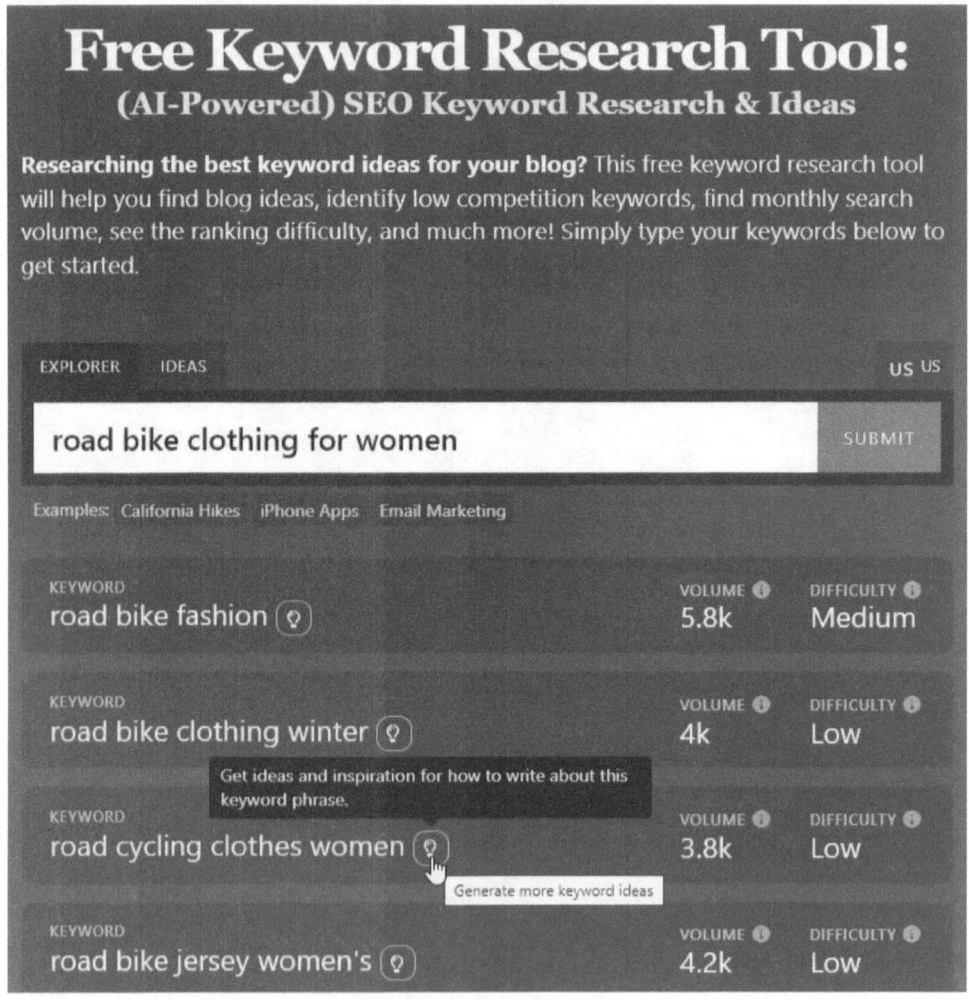

Figure 4: Road Bike Clothing for Women

Just by niching down a bit further, by adding the phrase "for women", we've uncovered some excellent ideas.

The 4 Things You Must Know
to Make Money While You Sleep

For example, "road cycling clothes (for) women" has 3,800 searches per month with low competition, so this is a keyword you can write an informative article about and direct your readers to relevant affiliate products.

Go ahead and do your own research.

Selecting a niche is examined in a lot more detail in Book 2 of the Internet Marketing FAST series *How to Select Your Internet Marketing Niche*.

You can claim the complete 8-book Internet Marketing FAST series when you register your interest in the training course at:

https://imfasttraining.com/expression-of-interest/

The 4 Things You Must Know
to Make Money While You Sleep

Second Thing: Register a Domain Name

Your Domain Name is Your Business Address

Figure 5: Your Domain Name

Just as a good street address is important to a bricks and mortar business, a good domain name is important to an online business.

But what makes a good domain name?

Well, first of all, it has to reflect your business. When a prospective visitor sees it, they should be in no doubt as to what your business is about.

In addition, these are the other desirable characteristics:

It should have a dot com extension

The shorter the better, as long as it still makes sense. All the single word domains are long gone, and most of the two-word ones. If you can summarize your story in three words and they're available as a .com domain name, that's great.

The 4 Things You Must Know
to Make Money While You Sleep

For example, if I wanted to create a website that was all about coffee (a very popular subject) and use affiliate links to sell associated product, including high ticket items like fully automatic coffee machines, here are some domain names I could be investigating:

allcoffeelovers.com

thecoffeebarista.com

thedailygrind.com

coffeeforall.com

You just need a bit of imagination and just keep coming up with variations until you find one that no one else has thought of.

Sticking with the cycling clothing idea examined previously I went to Namecheap and checked out roadbikeclothing.com for availability.

At the time of writing, roadbikeclothing.com was available for registration.

As a new customer, you would be able to get it for just $5.98 for one year's registration by using the coupon mentioned on the page.

The 4 Things You Must Know
to Make Money While You Sleep

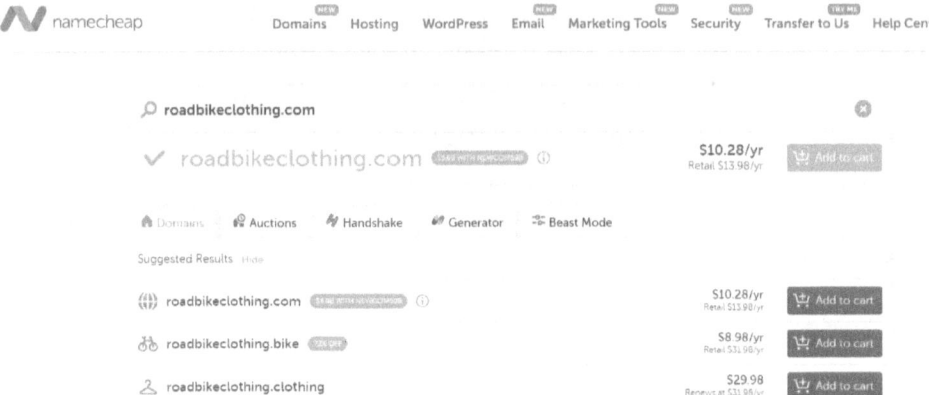

Figure 6: Domain Name Available

This would be a great domain name for a website specializing in Road Bike Clothing.

The 4 Things You Must Know
to Make Money While You Sleep

What Are All These TLDs (Top Level domains)?

Figure 7: Top Level Domains

The 4 Things You Must Know
to Make Money While You Sleep

TLDs (Top Level Domains) are what appears to the right of the dot in your domain name.

The name you've chosen, that appears to the left of the dot, is called an SLD (Second Level Domain).

Originally, there were just three TLDs.

.com was for commercial websites like yours.

.org was for non-profit or charitable websites.

.net was for everything else on the internet. Then .info was added for sites designed to inform and educate.

Since then, there have been a proliferation of TLDs, such as .biz, .pro, .tv and so on, with new ones being constantly added. This has happened partly because of the explosion of websites, to make more possibilities available, but also simply because the more available, the more potential profit there is for the domain name registrars.

However, this has also resulted in the .com version becoming more and more valuable and highly regarded.

The upshot is simply this. Get a .com domain for your website.

The 4 Things You Must Know

to Make Money While You Sleep

How to Register a Domain Name

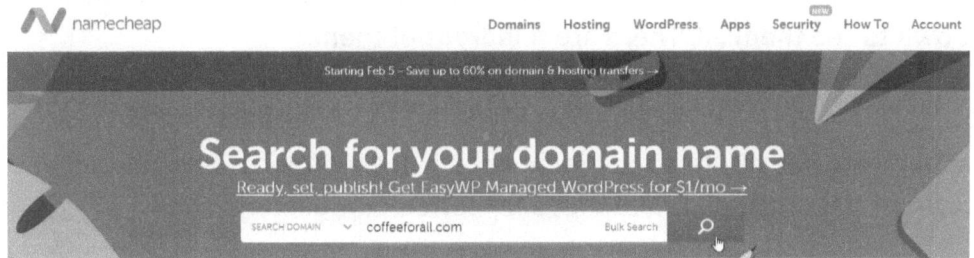

Figure 8: Search for Your Domain Name

Enter the domain you want and press Enter or click on the Search icon.

I've entered one of the coffee-oriented domains we considered earlier.

Namecheap will tell me if coffeeforall.com is available.

Figure 9: Domain Name Not Available

The 4 Things You Must Know
to Make Money While You Sleep

As expected, this particular domain name isn't available.

Namecheap will tell you what other TLDs are available and you can scroll down to see them all. There are hundreds of them.

But we are only interested in the .com, so let's try some other possibilities.

What if we substituted youandme for all? It's a bit long, but not bad and rolls off the tongue easily. So let's try coffeeforyouandme.com.

Figure 10: Successful Domain Name Search

And there we have it, a successful domain name search. We could continue searching from here or we could decide to go with this one by clicking on *add to cart* and paying $10.28 (or $5.98 if you're a new customer) for a year's registration.

Note: coffeeforyouandme.com was available when this book was written. It may not be available now.

Namecheap Domain Name Registrar

You've seen how you can use Namecheap to check out possible domain names until you find one that you're happy with. Then register and purchase for just $5.98.

You can go to Namecheap HERE.

The 4 Things You Must Know
to Make Money While You Sleep

Use Domain Wheel for Inspiration

A useful tool to help you research domain names is https://domainwheel.com/.

Open Domain Wheel in one tab and Namecheap in another.

Enter your seed word into Domain Wheel, check only the .com extension and click *Search Domain*.

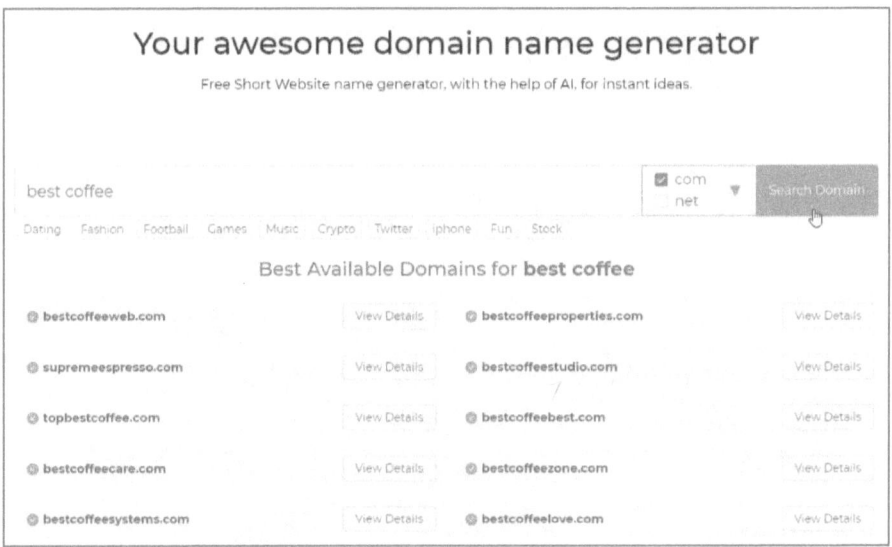

Figure 11: Domain Name Generator

If you don't see a suitable domain name, try a different seed word.

When you find a good name, go to Namecheap and register it.

The 4 Things You Must Know
to Make Money While You Sleep

Figure 12: Register the Domain You Found

Third Thing: Open a Web Host Account

What is a Website Host?

Figure 13: Web Hosting and Domain Hosting

A website host is a computer connected to the internet where your website is stored. When someone enters your website's domain name into a search engine, the search engine retrieves your website's details from the website host and displays them.

The 4 Things You Must Know

to Make Money While You Sleep

Domain Name Host

In Your Domain Name is Your Business Address on page 20 we looked at using a domain name host.

A domain name host like Namecheap holds all of the details of your new domain name and most importantly, translates the human-readable address domainname.com into the actual digital address where your website is stored. This is referred to as your DNS (Domain Name Server).

Web Host

Domain Name Hosts will frequently offer web hosting as well.

I really prefer to keep the two separate and independent.

SiteGround

I recommend using SiteGround as your web host. They use fast, 100% reliable servers and their support is excellent.

What Does SiteGround Cost?

SiteGround has three service levels and corresponding pricing.

Startup

The Startup plan allows you to host one website and costs $4.99 per month, billed as $59.88 for 12 months. You can have up to 10,000 website visitors per month.

I don't recommend this, as you will want to build several internet marketing businesses, not just one. In addition, the higher plans offer more features.

The 4 Things You Must Know
to Make Money While You Sleep

GrowBig

The GrowBig plan allows you to host an unlimited number of websites and provides premium features. It costs $7.49 a month, billed as $89.88 for 12 months. You can have up to 100,000 website visitors per month.

This is the plan I recommend that you use. It will allow you to get several businesses up and running on a fast, reliable server at an economic price.

GoGeek

The GoGeek plan is for when you have a large number of businesses running and want the best possible facilities for them. It costs $12.49 a month, billed as $149.88 for 12 months. It caters for up to 400,000 visitors a month.

You'll know when you're ready for this!

What Do You Get with SiteGround?

- The fastest, most reliable web host servers available on the internet
- Choice of server location. Choose the ones geographically closest to your target market for the fastest load time possible
- Free SSL certificate for all your websites, so that they use https protocol, essential for Google trust
- One-click WordPress installation
- The best support in the business.

To sign up with SiteGround, or just to find out more, go to Check SiteGround Here.

The 4 Things You Must Know
to Make Money While You Sleep

Fourth Thing: Build a Website

WordPress

WordPress is arguably the best, easiest and most effective platform to build a commercial website on.

What used to be incredibly difficult has been made a lot easier with WordPress.

But many people still struggle with it.

Much of its strength comes from the huge number of themes and plugins that have been created to extend its functionality. Some are free. Many are not. They don't all co-exist peacefully. Some used to be good, but haven't been updated to work with later versions of WordPress. It's a bit of a minefield.

This guide will lead you through installing a basic WordPress site and turning it into an attractive front for your prospective business.

I can't possibly cover all of the variables inherent in all the different domain name hosts, web hosts, themes and plugins that are available. All of the examples used in this document are based on my recommendations. Namecheap for domain name hosting, SiteGround for web hosting and Thrive for themes and plugins.

The 4 Things You Must Know
to Make Money While You Sleep

Pointing Your Domain Name to Your Host's DNS

When someone enters your domain name into a web browser like Google or Bing, it has to find your web host to bring up your website. Your web host and your domain name host must be linked.

This is achieved by entering your web host's DNS (Domain Name Servers) into your domain name details at your domain name host's website. This is a one-time job.

If you used Namecheap as recommended for your domain name host, this is how you do it.

Sign into Namecheap

Sign into Namecheap using the credentials you established when you registered your domain name(s).

The 4 Things You Must Know

to Make Money While You Sleep

Figure 14: Sign in to Namecheap

Then click on *Domain List*.

The 4 Things You Must Know
to Make Money While You Sleep

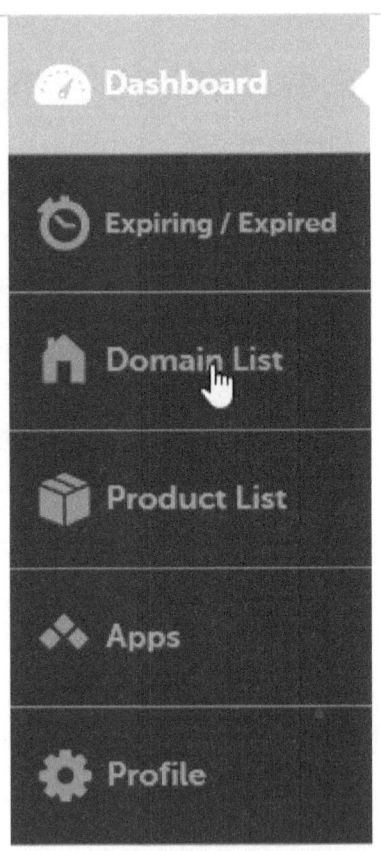

Figure 15: Click on Domain List

The 4 Things You Must Know
to Make Money While You Sleep

Select the Domain to be Updated

Click the check box next to the domain name to be edited then the drop-down labelled *Actions* and select *DNS / Host Records*.

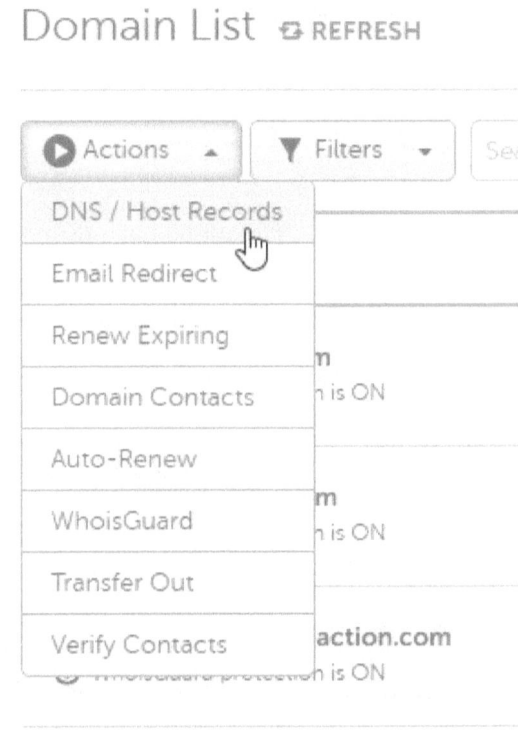

Figure 16: Select the Domain Name

On the next screen, click the check boxes that say you know what you're doing and then the *Next* button.

Enter Your Web Host's Name Servers

Check the radio button Custom DNS and enter your web host's domain name servers.

The 4 Things You Must Know
to Make Money While You Sleep

To find out your name servers, go to SiteGround and click on Site Tools for your website.

Figure 17: Siteground Nameservers

Your nameservers for that site are listed under Site Information.

In the example above, they are

ns1.siteground.net and

ns2.siteground.net.

Go to Namecheap to enter them into the relevant domain name details.

Select your domain name, click on the drop-down to the right and select Manage.

In the Name Servers section, select Custom DNS and enter the nameservers from Siteground.

The 4 Things You Must Know
to Make Money While You Sleep

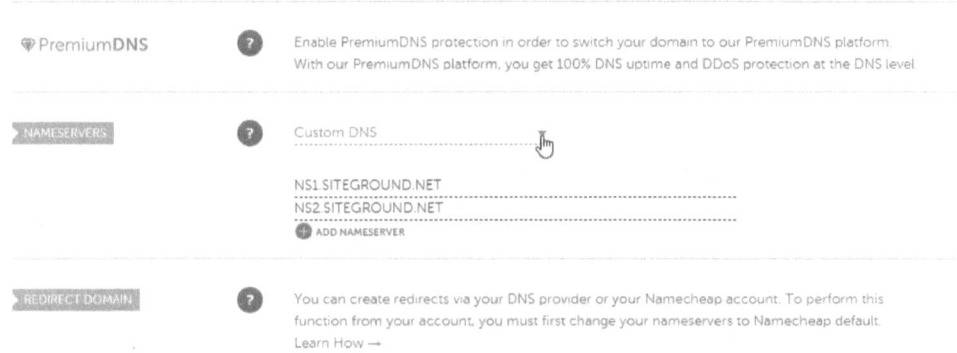

Figure 18: Update the Name Servers

Save and Propagate

Then click on the green tick in the Nameservers section to update the change.

Note that this doesn't happen immediately because there are servers all over the world that need to be updated. This is called propagation. Although you will be told to allow up to 48 hours, it normally only takes a few hours.

After a little while, you will be able to install WordPress at your web host.

If you are not using Namecheap as your domain name host, the procedure will be different, but the principle is the same. Similarly, if you are not using SiteGround as your web host, the name servers will also be different.

Installing WordPress

Creating a new WordPress site at SiteGround is quick and easy. I've covered it in detail in Book 4 in this series *How to Host Your Website*.

The 4 Things You Must Know

to Make Money While You Sleep

Modifying the Basic Setup

There are a couple of things you should do to modify the basic WordPress setup.

Trash the Default Post and Page

In your site's WordPress back office, click on *Posts*. You will see the default WordPress post "Hello world!".

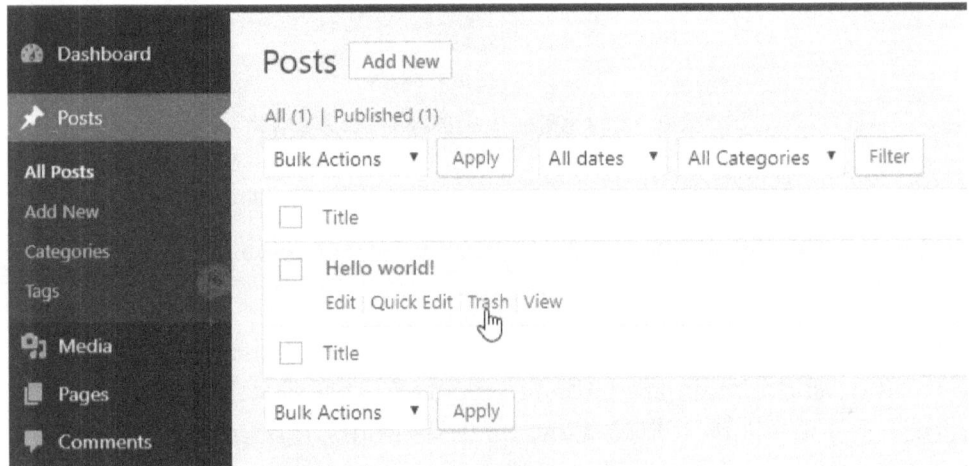

Figure 19: Trash the Default Post

Hover over the default post and click on *Trash*.

In your site's WordPress back office, click on *Pages*. You will see default WordPress pages such as "Privacy Policy" and "Sample Page".

The 4 Things You Must Know

to Make Money While You Sleep

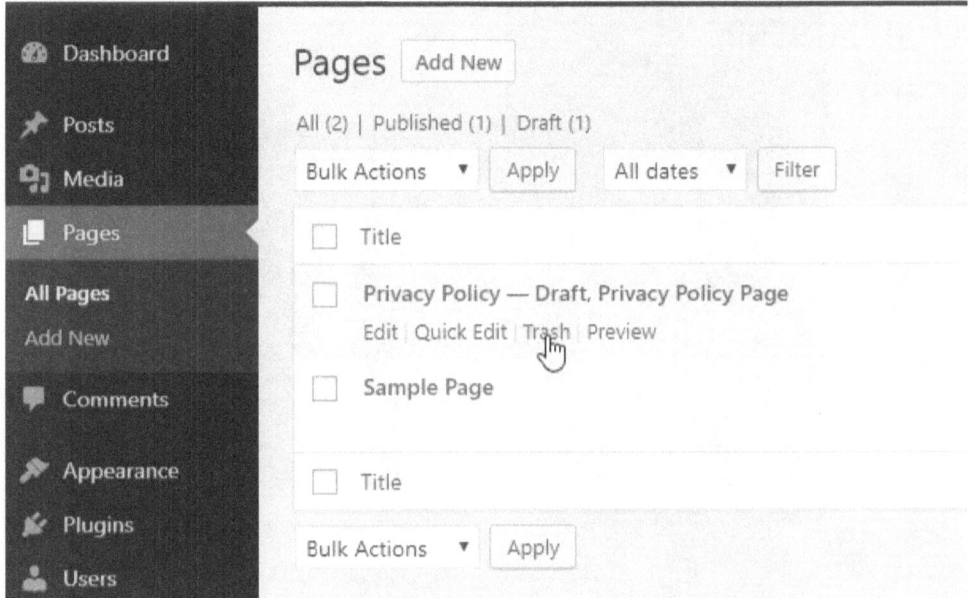

Figure 20: Trash the Default Pages

Hover over each of the default pages in turn and click on *Trash*.

You will be creating your own Privacy Policy page later.

Fix Site Identity

In the WordPress back office, click on *Appearance* then *Customize*.

The 4 Things You Must Know
to Make Money While You Sleep

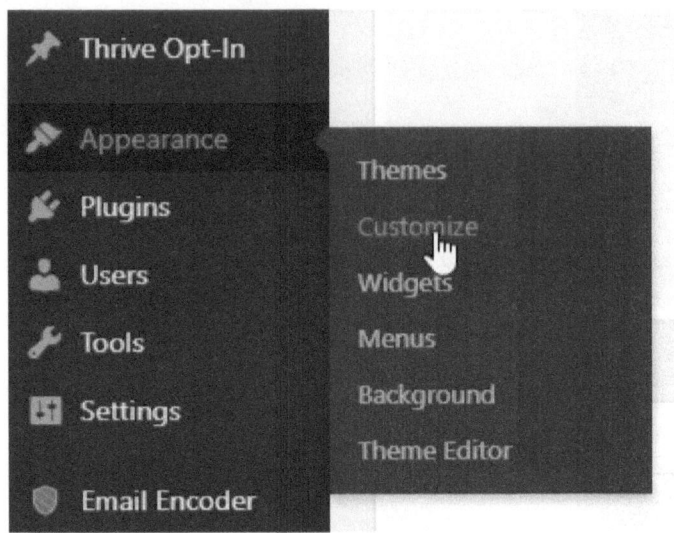

Figure 21: Click on Customize

Select Site Identity and complete Site Title and Tagline as appropriate for your site. You can always change these later.

Then click on the *Publish* button.

Clean up the Plugins
In the WordPress back office, click on *Plugins*.

The 4 Things You Must Know
to Make Money While You Sleep

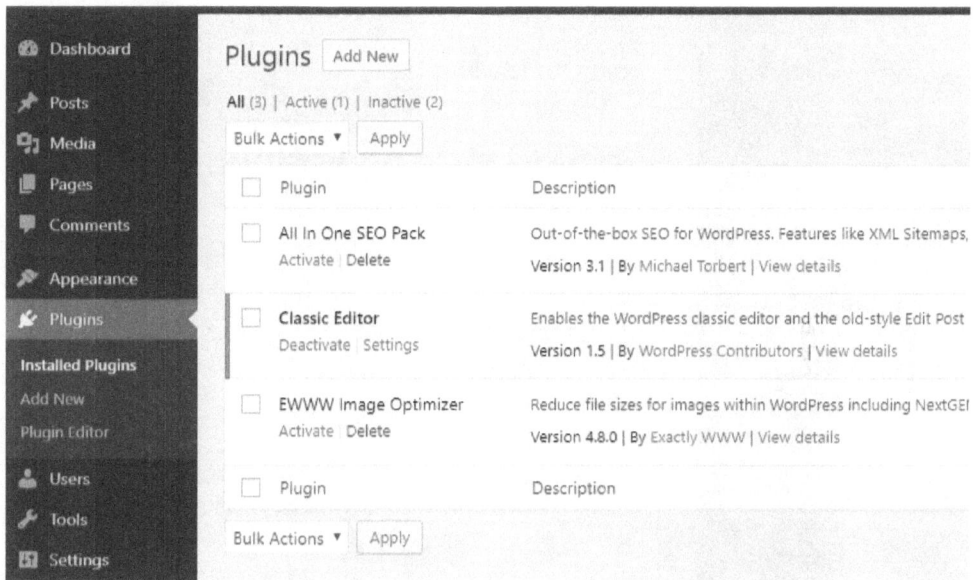

Figure 22: Initial Plugin Setup

Activate the All in One SEO Pack

Install the All in One SEO Pack as a new plugin. If you don't know how to do this, I've covered it in Book 5 in this series *WordPress for the Technically Challenged*.

It's an excellent plugin. Click *Activate* and then make the following adjustments:

Under All-in-One SEO, click on *Feature Manager* and activate the XML Sitemap.

The 4 Things You Must Know

to Make Money While You Sleep

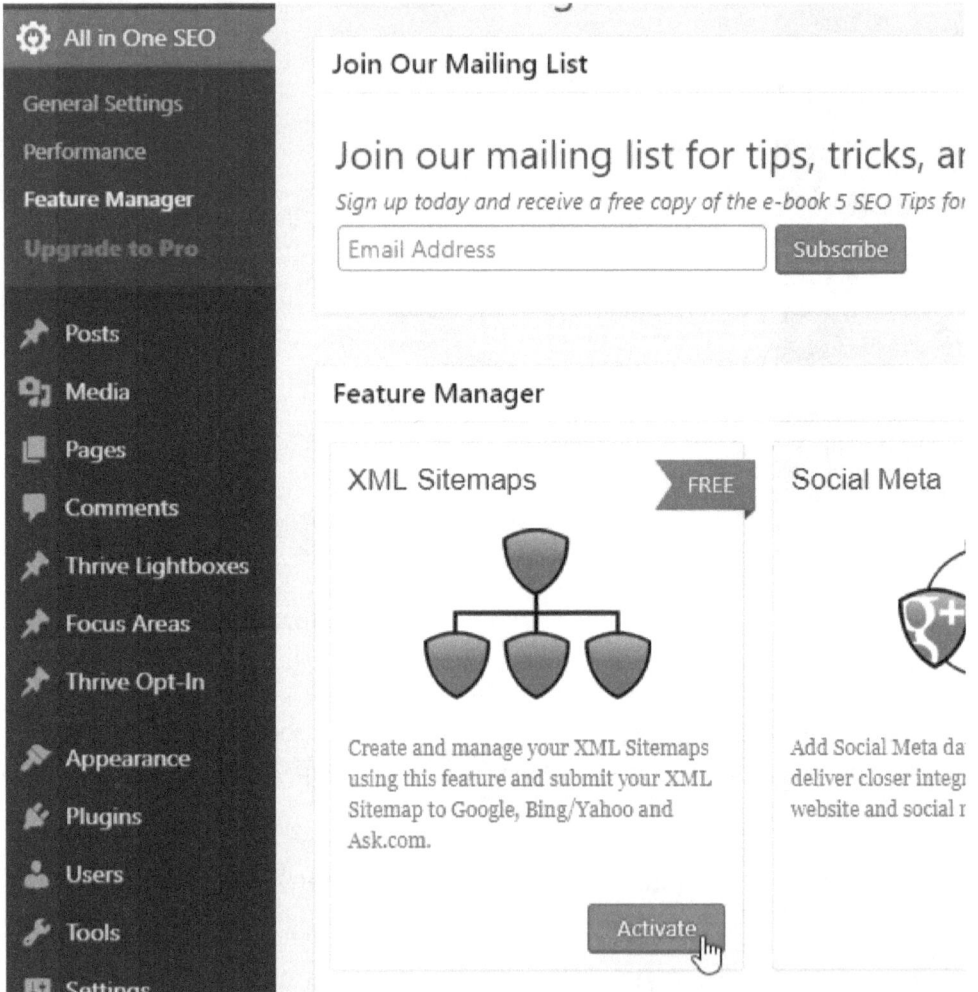

Figure 23: Activate XML Sitemap

There is no need to upgrade to the Pro version of All in One SEO Pack. The free version gives you all you need.

The 4 Things You Must Know

to Make Money While You Sleep

The Classic Editor.

Some time ago, WordPress introduced a new block editor called Gutenberg.

But they left the old Classic Editor in place, as many people didn't (and still don't) like the new one.

But if you've followed my recommendation to get Thrive Themes and Plugins, you can delete the WordPress Classic Editor as you'll have Thrive Architect, the best WordPress editor available.

Delete the EWWW Image Optimizer.

If you've followed my recommendation to get Thrive Themes and Plugins, you can delete the EWWW Image Optimizer as Thrive has a better one.

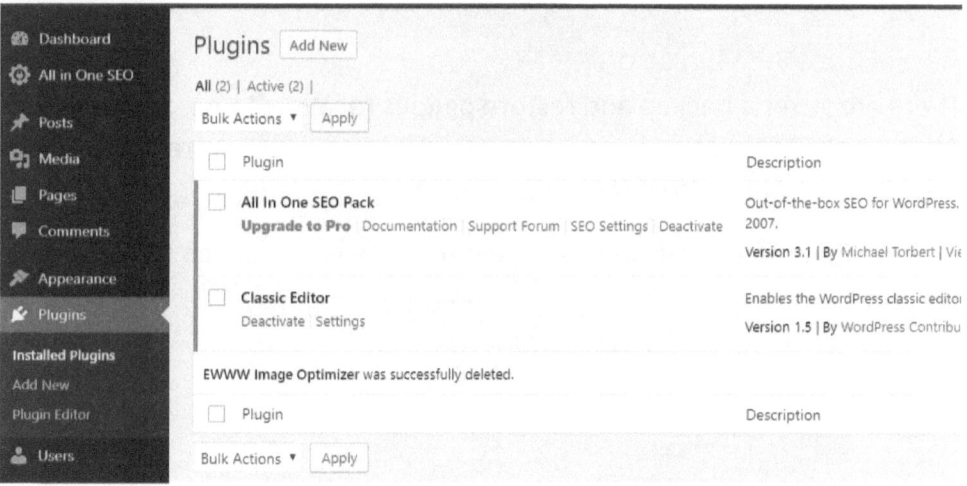

Figure 24: Plugins Updated

Install Backup and Restore

Most web hosts back up their hosted sites on a regular basis, typically daily. You don't see the backup; it's kept on their servers.

The 4 Things You Must Know

to Make Money While You Sleep

There are three reasons you shouldn't rely on that backup and need your own local one as well.

- The timing isn't under your control. If you've just put in several hours of painstaking work on your website that would be devastating to lose, you'll feel much better if you back it up immediately.
- Having your own backup means you can move to another web host easily if you wish. Just point the domain name at the new host, create an empty WordPress site and restore your backup file to it.
- What if you have an issue with your existing host? Financial, for example. Without your own backup, your host can hold your website to ransom. Particularly if they also host your domain name. With a local backup and your domain name hosted elsewhere, they have no control over you.

All in One WP Migration

There are several backup and restore plugins for WordPress. I recommend *All in One WP Migration* because I've used it to back up *and* restore several websites and I know that it works.

Click on Plugins >> Add New and then do a keyword search for *All in One WP Migration*.

The 4 Things You Must Know
to Make Money While You Sleep

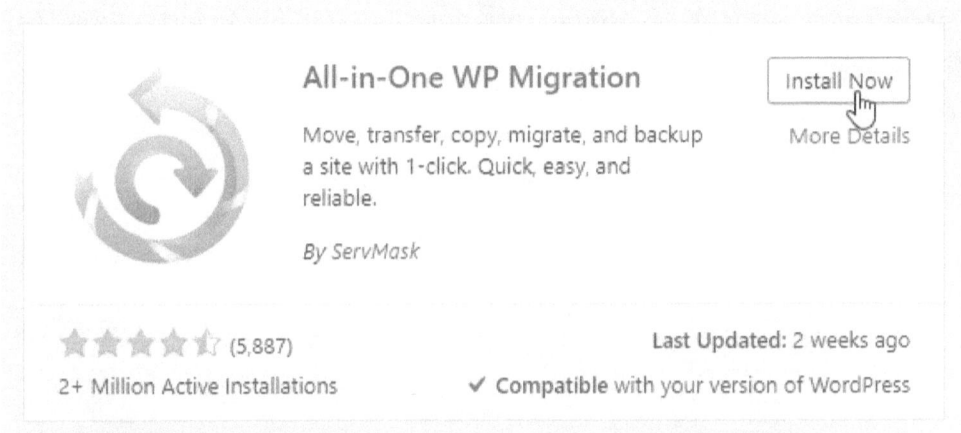

Figure 25: Install All in One WP Migration

Install the plugin and then Activate it.

Create Your First Backup
Once you've activated the plugin, it will appear as a new tool in the WordPress menu.

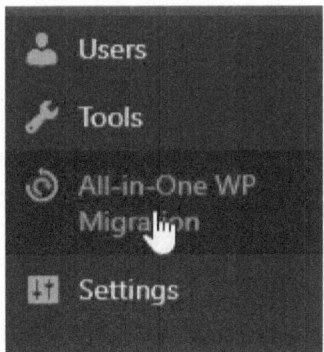

Figure 26: Backup Tool in WP Menu

Click on the menu item and then *Export* to create your first backup.

The 4 Things You Must Know
to Make Money While You Sleep

You have a number of options for your backup file's destination. My preference is as a file on my local computer.

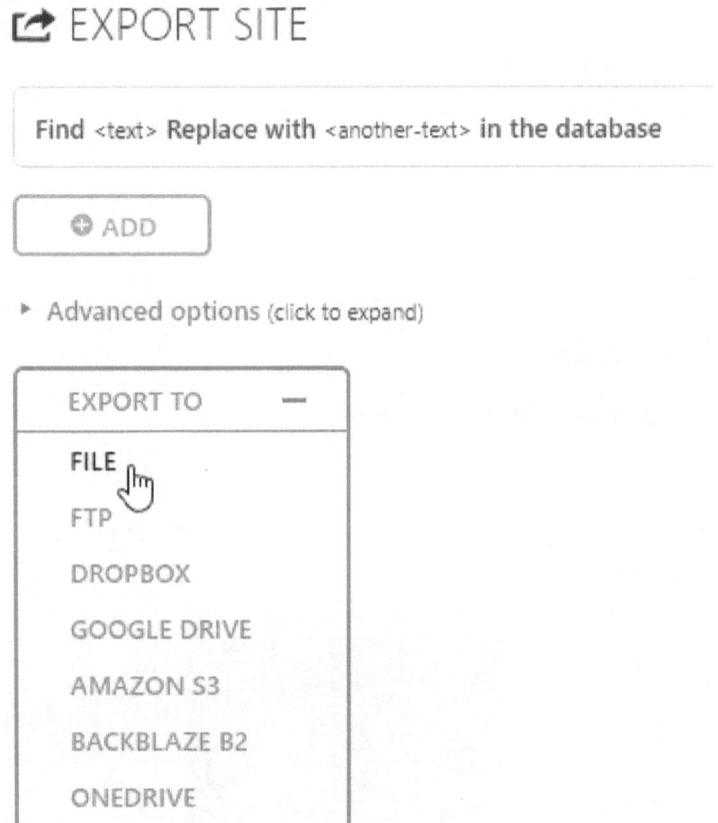

Figure 27: Select the Backup's Destination

Progress messages are displayed as the backup takes place, followed by a flashing invitation to download the file.

The 4 Things You Must Know
to Make Money While You Sleep

Click on the invitation and the backup file is downloaded into your Downloads folder, from where you can copy it to wherever you want to keep it permanently.

Creating a Logo

An attractive logo is an important part of your site's impact.

You can have a small logo, with your menu to the right or (my preference) a banner logo, spreading across the page with the menu underneath.

You can get either designed for a reasonable price at Fiverr (go to https://www.fiverr.com/ and search for logo design) or you can make your own.

You will need to find a suitable uncopyrighted image. There are a number of sites that provide these. My personal favorite is Pixabay (https://pixabay.com/). Their image quality is excellent and I can always find one that is suitable.

Then you need software that will allow you to trim, resize and add text to create your actual logo.

A tool that I've used for years and wouldn't be without is Snagit by TechSmith. Snagit is the king of screen capture software, but it also comes with an editor that you can use to create your logo. Have look at it here: https://techsmith.z6rjha.net/c/1375414/347799/5161.

The 4 Things You Must Know
to Make Money While You Sleep

The Rest of the Books

The *4 Things You Must Know* is the first book in my Internet Marketing FAST series.

Watch out for the rest, all available as both Kindle Singles and Paperbacks.

1. The 4 Things You Must Know (to Make Money While You Sleep)
2. How to Select Your Internet Marketing Niche
3. How to Register a Domain Name
4. How to Host Your Website
5. WordPress for the Technically Challenged
6. Building Your Website with Thrive
7. The Thrive User
8. The Thrive Expert

You can get the Kindle and Paperback links to the books on Amazon at

https://www.amazon.com/dp/B08QS6KPZY

The 4 Things You Must Know
to Make Money While You Sleep

About the Author

As an 80 year old (in 2024) fitness fanatic and successful internet marketer, Phil Lancaster is a bit of an anomaly.

Through a combination of bad luck and bad business decisions, he found himself broke and alone at 74.

Now, a few years later, he has several internet businesses that combine to bring him a 6-figure income.

It wasn't easy and he got burned a few times on the way, but he reckons that anyone can do it with the right road map.

He wants to help you to get started the way he did, but without making the same mistakes.

Anyone, from student to baby boomer (and older) can make money through the internet.

Phil's IM Fast series of mini-books will get you started. At just $2.99 (Kindle) or $7.99 (paperback) each, you won't find a better investment.

Or you can express your interest in his Internet Marketing FAST training course and qualify for free gifts at:

https://imfasttraining.com/expression-of-interest/